The Life Story
of

Halle
and
Lujah

'Passing the Wealth
to the next Generation'

BY ALVIN WAVERLEY BROWN JUNIOR

ILLUSTRATED BY JENIECE MITCHELL

To order additional copies of this book, contact:
Xlibris
844-714-8691
www.Xlibris.com
Orders@Xlibris.com

ISBN: Softcover   978-1-4653-3765-8
         EBook   978-1-6641-6598-4

Print information available on the last page

Rev. date: 03/26/2021

This book is dedicated to all God's parents and children.
May God's grace be with you all!

A special thanks to my adoptive parents,
Mr. Mike E. Offord and Ms. Martha Ann Brown Lee,
they have both gone home to be with the Lord.

To my Queen, Mrs. Regina Lynn Brown.
My Children; Alvin III., Latosha, Nicole, Joshua and Aljerett.
My Grandchildren; Krystiona, Marvin, Alvin IV., Jayla, Ja'da,
Taylor, Xavier, Antwann and Damariae.

To all of my friends, family, and to John and Dana Anthony for their unselfish
support, Thanks!

Bishop, Dr. Dale E Bronner and Dr. Nina Bronner Word of Faith Family
Worship Cathedral 212 Riverside Phwy Austell, GA 30168
"mailto:contact@woffamily.org" contact@woffamily.org 770-774-8840,
thank you for your perseverance and acting out of what God has
spoken to you. In you He lives. This Gospel has changed my
life forever, Amen.

Blessings to the Word of Faith Family!

Message to the Reader

Halle and Lujah paints a realistic picture of everyday situations, hardships, and "coming of age" issues that hit home to young teens with low self-esteem because of alienation at home or no family support system. Their story gives our young children and teens hope for a future, by showing them options on how to deal with their everyday problems. Luther and Christina Martin, as well as the twin's grandmother, prepared the children through a foundation of love, discipline and Biblical principles early in their lives.

Prayer changes things!

Suggestion Order of Prayer

Adoration

Confession

Thanksgiving

Supplication

Not so long ago and not so far away, Christina and Luther Martin were happily living on a small island named St. Davis, just west of Bermuda in the Virgin Islands.

One day, Mrs. Martin visited the doctor and was told that she was expecting a child.

She told Luther and right away, he ran out into the community to spread the good news. He was a very proud man.

Luther was an engineer who traveled as a salesman. While he was away on one of his trips,

Mrs. Martin returned to the doctor's office and learned that she was not expecting one child, but two! Mrs. Martin shouted, "HALLELUJAH!" She could hardly wait for Mr. Martin to return home to tell him the great news.

For the first time in the history of this island, twins were born. Luther and Christina never imagined that one would be a boy and the other a girl. Upon their births, the Martin's gave the naming of the children much thought. The girl would be named Halle and the boy would be named Lujah. They were indeed a very happy couple.

The children were born very healthy. As time went by, the twins grew up on the island adopting spiritual customs and spending much time discovering their surroundings and culture with their grandmother.

One day, Halle asked a question. "How can God really help us?" Her grandmother replied by saying, "Child, God will answer your prayers. You just pray and be obedient." Both Halle and Lujah had many questions about this big country they had always heard about, America, the land of opportunity.

Halle began to dream about going to America. She would always read magazines about the life styles in America. She wanted to go there to study and to live.

Mr. Martin discovered Halle's desire and told his wife Christina

"One day we will relocate to America and there I will work hard and build us a nice home, and the kids will get a better education."

When Luther returned to the office, after being away for several days, his boss said to him,
     "Luther, we are going to open a division in the United States and you will be relocating there as a Manager."
Luther was a very happy man.

Mr. Martin arrived home and told Mrs. Martin "At dinner, I'm going to tell you all of the great news I've learned today. I think we will be a very happy family."

    "My boss today asked me to relocate to America to head up a new division, and I said yes. Thank God our dream has come true."

More than anyone else, Halle was the happiest. The dreamer's dream came true.

At the airport, the pastor and the family gathered around in a circle holding hands, touching in agreement. The pastor began to pray.

"Father in the name of our Lord and Savior Jesus Christ, we gather here today with this family in need of protection, peace, and harmony. Let your will be done in each of their lives as it is in heaven. Father keep them in their going and coming, in the name of our Lord and Savior we ask, Hallelujah Amen."

They arrived in America. There was so much
to do after settling into their new home.

Halle and Lujah were enrolled in school
and they soon made many new friends.

The guys in school began to call Lujah "Rasta Man". Rasta Man is Reggae lingo that Americans affectionately label those from the islands. Lujah thought about his nickname for a while. He felt it was okay for the American guys to call him "Rasta Man" since it was done in good spirit.

Lujah was playing the guitar during music class one day, and everyone begin talking about his talent.

"Hey man, my name is Tony, what's yours?"

"Lujah," he replied. Tony asked,

"Would you like to sit in with us tomorrow night? I'm organizing a band to participate in the school's talent search!" Lujah said,

"No man, I need to study, so I think I'll pass."

Halle and Lujah were so excited to be in America. They were full of joy. At this point, Halle wanted them to focus on their careers. Her dream was to become a counselor in the local church ministry and Lujah's dream was to be Minister of Music. She hoped her brother would stay focused on their childhood dreams.

Nevertheless, the guys kept on asking Lujah to come over and practice, and he finally said,

"Well, let me ask my parents and I'll get back with you guys tomorrow."

This was a turning point for Lujah to make a decision right on the spot. Instead of him making the decision, he was able to resist the peer pressure by telling the guys "Let me ask my parents."

Lujah went home to talk with his parents about what the guys had asked.

Lujah said, "Dad, would it be alright to sit in with the band tomorrow night?"

Luther talked it over with his wife and daughter at dinner and answered,

"Lujah it's fine with us, but how will you get home son?" Lujah replied, "One of the guys will bring me back home."

Lujah returned to school and told them, "Yeah Mon, I will come over tonight and play with you guys. Could you give me a ride home afterwards?" They said, "Sure man."

Lujah went over and "sat-in" with the guys. He was the most awesome guitar player the guys had ever met. They said,

"Hey Lujah, you have got to play with us in the school talent search. We will blow everyone away. Nobody can beat us! We can get a lot of recognition and maybe we can even get a record deal."

Lujah returned home and told his family, "This evening was great and they liked the way I played." The family was excited. As he continued to talk, Lujah cast a glance at his sister and noticed that she dropped her head as if she knew that he would soon be going in another direction in his life.

Live concert performance at the
school talent search.

Lujah and his band received the first place award at the school talent search.

Halle began to watch her brother. At that moment, she began to drift away in her spirit, she knew her brother would not be about their Father's business. Lujah was crowded around by all of the fans. People were asking him to play nightclubs and special engagements. Of course this being new to Lujah, he was all for it.

Lujah and the band had landed a contract with a recording label. The band had their first live recording and soon afterwards they were touring nationwide.

Halle didn't know what to do. She felt withdrawn and began to blame herself for wanting to come to America. Lujah had parted from her life and she returned to the most powerful place in the world, the church altar. Halle remembered what her grandmother told her about prayer when she was a little girl and she began to pray this prayer, "Spirit of the living God, come now in to our lives and touch my brother Lord, wherever he may be. Thank you Holy One, Amen......"

One night after a concert, Lujah fell down to his knees and began to pray, asking God to forgive him for backsliding.

"Lord Jesus please forgive me for departing from my family. Please pour your Spirit back into me. I surrender myself completely in every area of my life to you, Amen."

As the doors of the church opened, Lujah walked down the aisle and gave his life back to Christ. The church began to praise and worship in a mighty way.

The Martin family reunited. Halle and Lujah presumed their careers in the ministry. They lived happily ever after.

Proverbs 22:6 K.J.V.

Train up a child in the way he should go: and when he is old, he will not depart from it.

"THE 3 T's"

TRAIN up a child in the way they should go,
When they get older they will know, grow,
And take it in everyday,
They will never go astray.
When you train, you teach,
They learn and obey,
And their skies will never go gray,
They will know what's the right way.
TRAIN, TALK, AND TREASURE
TALK to your child and communicate well,
Don't yell,
Just listen to what's on their mind,
Be diverting and spend a little time,
Talk to your parents, give them a hug and kiss,
When you are older, you'll want to reminisce.
Talking to God will make things right,
Let God handle your battles that's not your fight!
Talking will make things flow at an equal rate,
Talk, Listen, and please Communicate!
TRAIN, TALK, AND TREASURE
TREASURE your love and never let it go,
The more you cherish it, the bigger it will grow,
Love one another and always show you care,
Be there, and nothing will despair, and
Everything will go well!
Treasure the love God has given you from up above,
And show the world you are somebody to be proud of!
TRAIN, TALK, AND TREASURE!

- Marshetta English

Duties of the Parents to the Children

Create and altar in your home. Have prayer there morning and nights together.
The altar you make for me. Exodus: 22, 24-25 N.L.T.

Discuss differences with your children at dinner. on a regular basic, "Kids are people too". Father it's okay to discipline your children and then express your love the next day.

When discipline is administered by either parent, the parent not disciplining the child should be in total support. Contradiction creates division in the household.

Mothers should have regular talks with their daughters about womanhood and sexual relationship with boys. Relax, better you then some one else.

Children must be introduced to our Lord and Savior at a very early age by the way of Sunday School. This will make life easier for you and the school teachers.

Parents, when your spiritual father talks about establishing principle values in the home, it's o.kay, to do so you are the head, not the tail.

'Fathers, provoke not your children to anger
lest they be discouraged.'
Colossians 3:21 K.J.V.

Duties of the Children to the Parents

Children, obey your parents in the Lord for this is right. Honor thy father
and mother, which is the first Commandment with promise;
That it may be well with thee, and thou mayest live long on earth.
Ephesians 6: 1-3 K.J.V.

Always have an open conversation with your parents about any and everything.
It's okay, they have the answers that will see you through.

Children, seek God with all your heart, you can depend on Him for everything in your life, Look at the world around us, the world we live in depends on Him too.

Now therefore hearken unto me, O ye children: for blessed are they that
keep my ways. Hear instruction, and be wise, and refuse it not.
Proverbs 8:32-33 K.J.V.

Children remember you are a gift to your parents. The discipline you receive, you may not approve of it all the time, but it's only to help you be all you can be in life. Obedience is the key, not disciplinary action.

Children when your parents give you a chore, it's your responsibility to perform it to the best of your ability. Guess what, it will build character in you.

These things, which you have both learned, and received, and heard, and
seen in me, do: and the God of peace shall be with you.
Philippians 4:9 K.J.V.

Alvin Waverley Brown Jr. is a multi-talented entrepreneur who resides in Atlanta, Georgia with his wife and youngest son. He truly understands the meaning of family and the importance of a good environment to raise children, which is why he chose Atlanta to nurture his family. At the tender age of 16 weeks, Mr. Brown was adopted by his neighbors. His adoptive parents loved him extremely and instilled in him the virtue to create his own "destiny attitude", which became the trademark of his infectious character. He has masterfully used his loving attitude and tenacious spirit to raise five children, who range in age from 12 years to 30. Mr. Brown also has five grandchildren, which includes a set of twins.

When asked why he wanted to write children's books, his response was "To instill high moral standards in today's youths." He continued by saying, "I remember when I was around six or seven years old, my parents and I would travel from church to church singing gospel songs with hopes of filling the listeners' hearts with joy. I also remember that my parents were entrepreneurs and avid churchgoers. They made sure that I received spiritual fulfillment and spiritual guidance. Collaboratively, all of these things kept my dream machine alive while most people's dreams die in early adulthood."

Mr. Brown would like for this book to be enjoyed by children and adults alike. In its teaching of valuable life lessons like the Parables of Christ, this book can be used to develop an intriguing common ground that youths can identify with. This particular story coincides with life's truism, such as a parent's intent for a better standard of living for their children. It includes youthful banter such as name-calling and a child's desire to be accepted by their peers while at the same time providing subtle and easily applied solutions to these and other youthful challenges. Mr. Brown uses the plush tropical surroundings and the bright colorful apparel of the islands to capture the readers' attention. The siblings' adventures in this story show how intoxicating the allure of fame and fortune can be, even to the best prepared. But it also shows that in the end, family, faith, hope, and love conquer all.

Mr. Brown hopes you and your children enjoy reading this book as much as he enjoyed writing it.

May all your days be blessed.